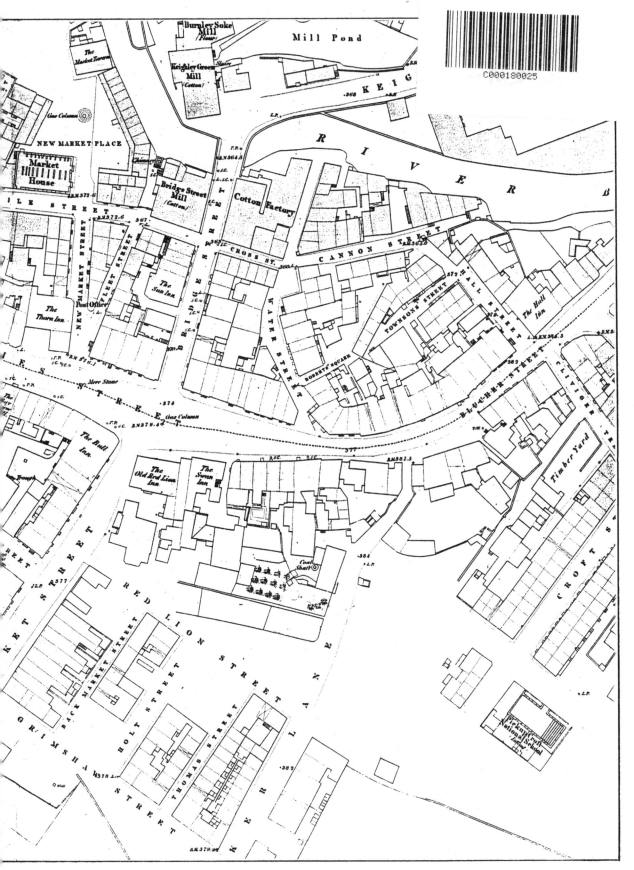

Detail from an Ordnance Survey map of 1851.

BURNLEY
A Pictorial History

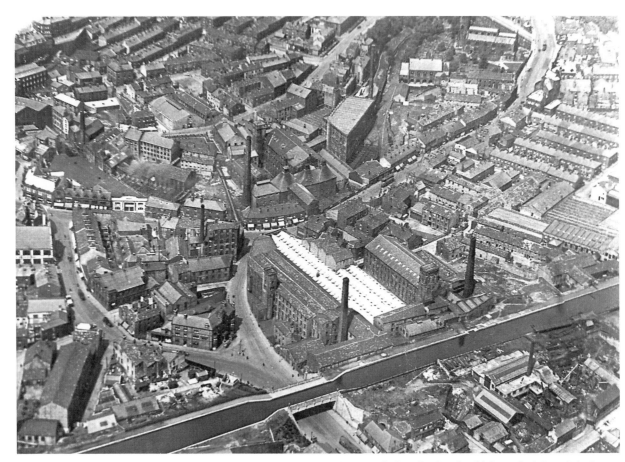

Aerial view of Burnley Centre, *c.*1930. In the top right corner can be seen St Peter's church which marked the original centre of the town. In the foreground is the embankment carrying the Leeds and Liverpool Canal, with the aqueduct over Yorkshire Street. Almost all the buildings in this photograph have now been demolished.

BURNLEY
A Pictorial History

Brian Hall and Ken Spencer

Phillimore

1993

Published by
PHILLIMORE & CO. LTD.
Shopwyke Manor Barn, Chichester, Sussex

ISBN 0 85033 866 2

Printed and bound in Great Britain by
BIDDLES LTD.
Guildford, Surrey

List of Illustrations

Frontispiece: Aerial view of Burnley Centre, *c.*1930

Acknowledgements

Most of the photographs and other illustrations are from the collection in the Burnley Central Library, and the authors' own collections. Nos. 8, 9, 12, 35, 56, 95 and 107 are reproduced by courtesy of Towneley Hall Art Gallery and Museums; no. 42 by courtesy of Roger B. Frost; no. 142 by courtesy of Althams Travel Services.

The authors would like to thank the staff of Burnley Central Library, Reference Dept. for their assistance in producing the book. They also acknowledge help from friends in the Burnley and District Historical Society, especially Barbara Bailey, Margaret Jones and James Howell.

Introduction

Burnley is situated at the confluence of two small rivers, the Brun and the Calder, in a valley almost completely surrounded by Pennine moorlands. It is on these moors that flint tools and weapons, left by the Stone-Age nomads who were the first inhabitants of the area, have been found. Here also is a significant number of Bronze-Age burial mounds, such as the one at Mosely Height which was excavated in 1950. The Celts of the Iron Age left several earthworks, and a number of place-names, such as Pendle, Calder and Ightenhill, but there is little evidence of any permanent settlement. Nor did the Roman occupation have much impact on the area.

After the Romans had abandoned Britain in A.D. 410, the country was invaded by barbaric tribes such as the Angles, who came into east Lancashire across the Pennines. Names such as Padiham and Habergham suggest that small groups of them had settled here by the early 7th century. but it is unlikely that there were any substantial settlements until *c*.800, when it is probable that the village which was to become Burnley was founded.

It was not until 1122 that the name Burnley, or Brunley as it was often written, appeared in a document—a charter granting the church of St Peter to the monks of Pontefract Priory. The name means 'the field by the Brun' or 'the brown field', and shows that a farming community had grown up around the church, protected by a loop in the river. Nearby were a number of other hamlets—Westgate, Fulledge, Healey and Towneley—which together made up the vill of Burnley.

The vill was part of the Honour of Clitheroe, which William the Conqueror granted to Roger of Poitou and which later passed into the hands of the De Lacy family. In 1294 Edward I granted to Henry de Lacy and his heirs a charter: '... that they have a weekly market on Tuesday in their manor of Bruneley in the County of Lancaster and a fair every year lasting through three days, that is on the eve, day and morrow of the Feast of the Apostles Peter and Paul'. The following year a market cross was put up near to the church, at a cost of 9s. 1d. A few years earlier a corn mill had been built and, in 1296, a fulling mill was established on the banks of the Brun; clearly Burnley was becoming a place of some importance.

By the 13th century, Burnley was part of the manor of Ightenhill, controlled from a manor house of which nothing remains, but whose site can be identified a short distance from the present Ightenhill Park Lane. Here, in 1323, King Edward II spent a few days; the first recorded royal visit to Burnley.

In the early 14th century, Burnley had about fifty families, mostly bondsmen, who worked the lord's land at Ightenhill and attended the halmot court in return for a few strips in the town field. There was also a number of free tenants including the Towneley and Stansfield families. As the century progressed, however, all the inhabitants became free, paying rent for their land but still observing the customs of the manor.

By the end of the Middle Ages the village of Burnley had well over one thousand inhabitants, and, as good agricultural land became scarce, people began to turn to other ways to eke out a meagre living, notably the manufacture of woollen cloth. More cottages were built, particularly in the area around St Peter's church, which became known as Top o' th' Town. After 1522 the halmot court was transferred to the church from Ightenhill Manor House, which then fell into disrepair.

The church itself was largely rebuilt in 1532 and two years later all the Burnley priests took the oath of allegiance to Henry VIII as Supreme Head of the church. When the chantries at the church were dissolved in the reign of Edward VI, the people of Burnley joined together to buy the chantry lands and gave them back to the former chantry priests. One of these had acted as schoolmaster and it soon became necessary for the chantry school to be re-endowed. As a result of this Burnley Grammar School was founded in 1559, the first headmaster being a former chantry priest, Gilbert Fairbank. In the early days it is probable that lessons were held in his house, but in 1602 one of the governors, John Towneley, paid for a new schoolhouse to be built in the churchyard.

Although the majority of Burnley inhabitants had accepted the new Protestant faith—in appearance at least—the Towneley family remained loyal to the Roman Catholic faith, and John himself paid more than £5,000 in fines and was imprisoned for many years for refusing to attend the Protestant services.

During the Civil War between Charles I and Parliament, the Towneley family were staunch Royalists. Charles Towneley was killed at the battle of Marston Moor, and there is a story that Oliver Cromwell helped Mrs. Towneley to search for the body of her husband on the battlefield. Most of the people in the Burnley area sided with Parliament and Colonel Richard Shuttleworth of Gawthorpe was in command of the local militia, who were involved in action against the Royalists at a number of places, including skirmishes at Read Old Bridge and Haggate.

During the 17th century Burnley developed into a small market town. As trade increased the market was extended and six cattle fairs were held each year. In 1617, a new market cross was erected and at about the same time a market house was built nearby. The woollen industry became increasingly important as some weavers began to work full time rather than plying their trade in addition to farming activities.

Changes also took place in agriculture when the commons of Burnley were enclosed between 1617 and 1622, thereby bringing the old open-field system of farming to an end. By this time over half the land was owned by six families, who leased to tenant farmers the land they themselves did not use. Manorial administration of the area changed, and responsibility passed to the officers of townships of Burnley, Habergham Eaves, Briercliffe and Cliviger. The officers—the churchwardens, surveyor of the highways, and overseer of the poor—were elected annually at the vestry meeting of the inhabitants held in St Peter's church.

It was during the 18th century that Burnley saw the beginning of the changes that were to turn it into an industrial town. The domestic system of manufacturing, in which woollen cloth was made in the workers' homes, was already well established. Sometimes the weaver worked for himself, buying the raw wool and selling the finished cloth, but more often he was employed by a clothier who paid him a wage for his work. As the century progressed, the work was sometimes carried out in a 'shed' or 'factory' belonging to the master. Burnley's earliest factories were a cloth-mill, dye-house and fulling mill built between 1736 and 1741, near to the confluence of the rivers Calder and Brun.

At first, water provided the motive power for the newly-invented machinery—the 'spinning-jenny', 'water-frame' and 'spinning-mule'—but in 1790 a steam engine was used for the first time in Burnley, in a new mill built by the Peel family. It was at this time, also, that cotton began to take over from wool as Burnley's main product.

With the industrial revolution came an increased demand for coal, which had been mined in the area since the mid-15th century from drift mines and bell-pits. Deeper shafts were sunk and by the end of the century there were more than a dozen pits in the centre of Burnley. There was also a number of iron foundries which were to play an increasingly important role as the textile industry developed.

The changes were well summed up in the entry in a 1792 directory:

> Burnley is a market town, situate in a rich and pleasant valley on the margin of the River Calder to the south and the River Brown to the north ... There are two fulling mills, a corn mill, and one for grinding wood and other materials for dyeing; also several engines for preparing and carding wool and cotton for spinning, worked by these streams ... By the spirited exertions of the woollen manufacturing, together with a prodigious quantity of worsted and cotton goods manufactured in the town and neighbourhood, it is greatly enriched and enlarged, and become a thriving and populous town.

At first it was only spinning which was carried out in factories, for although a power-loom had been invented in 1785, it was inefficient and slow to be adopted. Weaving continued to be done mainly by hand and even as late as 1830 there were far more handloom weavers than factory weavers. By the beginning of the 19th century the new spinning mills were producing large quantities of yarn and weavers were at a premium, often becoming quite prosperous. It was at this time that many of the stone-built weavers' cottages in the area were erected, some of which still exist on the outskirts of the town, such as those at Briercliffe.

Eventually, as power looms were improved and became more efficient, weaving sheds were added to many of the spinning mills and by 1850 there were some 9,000 looms in the town. From the 1840s many factories were built on the banks of the canal, the water from which could be used in the boilers, particularly in the area now known as the 'Weavers' Triangle'. Many factory owners leased out 'room and power', so that anyone with a minimum of capital could become a manufacturer. However, this system led to frequent bankruptcies and later in the century many mills were taken over by limited liability companies.

Other problems which beset the industry were the cotton famine of the 1860s, caused by the American Civil War, and frequent disputes over wages which often led to strikes, the most serious being the Weavers' Strike of 1878, which was accompanied by rioting.

After 1880, Burnley began to concentrate on weaving rather than spinning. This change was due to the introduction of ring-spinning in the cotton-towns of south Lancashire, which made it cheaper for local manufacturers to buy yarn rather than spin their own. The changeover was so rapid that Burnley was soon claiming to weave a greater length of cloth each year than any other town in the world, and by the early years of the 20th century there were in the region of 100,000 looms in the town.

As the manufacture of cotton grew, so did the allied industries of textile-engineering and coal-mining. The number of foundries producing steam engines and textile machinery increased and the 'Burnley loom' was recognised as one of the best of its kind. New and deeper coal mines were sunk and they all contributed to Burnley's growing importance as an industrial town.

The development of industry and trade from the 18th century meant that urgent improvements in transport became necessary. From the middle of the 16th century each parish was responsible for maintaining the highways, but attention to repairs was poor and most roads were little more than dirt tracks and often impassable in bad weather. Such roads were completely unsuitable for the transport of both raw material and the products of industry resulting in turnpike trusts being set up to build new roads and charge tolls for their use. The first trust in the Burnley area was established in 1754 to build a road from Blackburn to Colne and Addingham.

However, the transportation of goods remained slow and expensive until the end of the century when the Leeds and Liverpool Canal reached Burnley. Begun in 1770, the canal was not fully opened until 1816; the section through the town proved one of the most expensive to build, with the Burnley embankment costing £22,000 and Gannow tunnel £10,000. Canals were particularly cheap and convenient for carrying heavy and bulky goods, and occasionally carried passengers. They were, however, too slow for regular passenger transport which continued to be provided by stagecoaches until the coming of the railways.

In 1848, the East Lancashire Company's line from Accrington to Colne reached Burnley. It was followed a year later by one to Todmorden and, in 1876, by another to Blackburn via Padiham. The development of railways led to the immediate decline of long-distance road transport, but the Leeds and Liverpool Canal suffered less than most others from railway competition and continued to be a significant carrier of heavy goods.

As the town grew in size, the provision of local public transport became a necessity and, in 1879, the Burnley and District Steam Tramway Company was founded. The tramways were soon electrified and extended to link up with other towns. They continued in use until they were gradually superseded by motor buses in the 1920s, being finally withdrawn from service in 1935.

The development of industry brought immense changes to the appearance of the town and to the lives of its inhabitants. In 1801 Burnley was a market town with a population of just under 4,000; by 1851 it had grown into an industrial centre with almost 21,000 inhabitants. Attracted by the new factories, families moved into the town from surrounding villages, West Yorkshire, Rossendale and further afield. The need to provide homes for the workers led to the proliferation of low-cost housing in back-to-back terraces and courts, tenements and cellar dwellings, where over-crowding and inadequate water supply and sanitation led to frequent outbreaks of smallpox, cholera and typhoid fever.

Conditions in the factories were usually no better than those at home. The mills were badly ventilated and crowded with unguarded machinery. Hours were long,—between twelve and eighteen hours a day was common—and wages were barely above subsistence level. Children were frequently employed, some as young as seven. As the century progressed, working conditions were regulated by Acts of Parliament, but these were disliked by the employers, and even by many of the workers who feared that shorter hours would lead to lower wages.

Sometimes the workers took matters into their own hands and there were disturbances, such as the loom-breaking riots of 1826, and the plug riots which accompanied the demands for the People's Charter in the 1840s. By the second half of the 19th century, however, Burnley was entering into its period of greatest prosperity as the cotton trade began to expand, and this led to a rise in wages and some improvement in workers' conditions.

Another factor in the improvement of the town was the development of local government. At the beginning of the 19th century local affairs were still run by a number of unpaid officials elected at the annual vestry meeting. After 1817, however, the meeting appointed a 'town committee' who were to deal with police, poor relief, lighting and public health. Two years later an Act of Parliament was passed setting up a board of commissioners to run the town, but for some reason the Act was never implemented and the town committee continued to run local affairs.

Also in 1819, the Burnley Water Act was passed, under which a company was formed to supply piped water to the town, and in 1823 the Burnley Gas Company was formed. A private market company was set up which built a market hall on a site not far from the present one. This marked a shift of the town centre from outside St Peter's church to near the bottom of the present Manchester Road, then known as Market Street.

Over the next two decades the town committee saw its responsibilities gradually eroded. In 1837 the newly created Board of Guardians took over the relief of the poor, while in 1840 the county magistrates became responsible for the policing of the town. Then in 1844 a new board was formed to look after the roads, leaving the vestry meeting with responsibility only for election of the churchwardens.

In 1846 the Burnley Improvement Act brought about a complete reorganisation of local government, which by now was in the hands of a bewildering number of committees, boards and companies. A body of 60 commissioners was to be elected by the rate-payers, and was to be responsible for 'the better paving, lighting, cleansing, regulating and improving the town, and for better supplying the inhabitants with gas and water'. Although the commissioners immediately began the work of repaving and draining the streets and took over the supply of water, they were soon criticised particularly because of high rates which, in 1853, were levied at one shilling in the pound.

By 1860 the population of Burnley had reached almost 30,000, and it was felt that the time had come for the town to achieve corporate status. Consequently, a petition was presented to Queen Victoria and, in 1861, a charter of incorporation was granted, creating the Borough of Burnley, with eight aldermen and 24 councillors. They met under the chairmanship of the first mayor, John Moore, in a room over the fire station, but later the municipal offices were set up in the Public Hall in Elizabeth Street, where they remained until the present Town Hall was opened in 1888. In the following year Burnley was given the new status of a County Borough, responsible for running all aspects of local affairs; powers it retained until the reorganisation of local government in 1974.

The development of local government led to the creation of many new amenities in the town, whilst control over the building of houses meant a gradual improvement in living conditions and, consequently, in health. Many of the sick and needy, however, continued to rely on charity for help, and the Victoria Hospital, opened in 1886, was paid for entirely by public subscription.

Meanwhile, under the Parliamentary Reform Act of 1867, Burnley had gained its own M.P. The first election was held in 1868, with the Liberal candidate, Richard Shaw, defeating General Sir James Yorke Scarlett by 382 votes. Among Burnley's best known M.P.s have been Jabez Balfour, who was eventually imprisoned for fraudulent company dealings, Dan Irving, the town's first Labour member, and the Rt. Hon. Arthur Henderson, Home Secretary in the first Labour government of 1924 and later Foreign Secretary.

As Burnley grew, many new places of worship were built to minister to the spiritual needs of the town. For centuries St Peter's had been the only church in Burnley, but by the early 19th century it was unable to cater for the rapidly increasing population and, during the incumbency of the Rev. Robert Mosley Master, six new churches were built in various parts of the town. In 1867, St Peter's itself was raised to the status of rectory; it had previously been a chapel-of-ease in the Parish of Whalley, although in practice it had all the responsibilities of a parish church. In 1890 the Burnley Rectory Act created the office of Sufragan Bishop of Burnley and, until 1977, St Peter's was the only parish in England with a rector who was also a bishop.

Meanwhile there had been considerable developments in Nonconformist religion in the town. From the early years of the 18th century there are records of houses being used as dissenters' meeting places and the first Baptist chapel in the area was built at Haggate in

1767. In 1784 John Wesley paid the first of several visits to Burnley and four years later a Wesleyan chapel was built at Keighley Green. During the 19th century the Nonconformists played an important part in ministering to the needs of the people and raising the moral tone of the town, whilst numerous chapels of all denominations were built.

The Roman Catholics, who had worshipped in the chapel at Towneley Hall often in secrecy and at the risk of their lives, also benefited from increasing religious tolerance. In 1817 a chapel was opened on Todmorden Road and in 1849 St Mary's church was built to cater for the increasing number of worshippers.

Religious organisations were also largely responsible for the development of popular education in Burnley in the early years of the 19th century. For over 300 years Burnley Grammar School had provided a classical education for the sons of the gentry and professional men, but the majority of people were denied the most basic schooling. Towards the end of the 18th century a number of Sunday schools was set up which taught reading and writing as well as religion. The first was associated with St Peter's church. Other denominations quickly followed suit and over 20 Sunday schools had been founded by about 1870 with others later.

The churches and chapels soon turned their attention to the provision of day schools, usually under the Church of England's Society for the Education of the Poor or the non-denominational British and Foreign Schools Society, and by the 1850s there were nine such voluntary schools in Burnley. A considerable number of private schools was also founded including dames' schools, ladies' seminaries and a commercial and mathematical academy.

The voluntary schools gave a basic education in the 'three Rs' and it was left to the grammar school to provide more advanced learning. Gradually the narrow classical curriculum was widened to include subjects more suited to an industrial town. During the 1870s a new school building was erected on Bank Parade and the governing body reorganised to include reresentatives of the Borough Council and the recently established Burnley School Board. The School Board was a result of the 1870 Education Act. One of its first actions was to insist that all Burnley children must attend school between the ages of five and thirteen and in the last decade of the century a number of Board Schools were founded to cater for the increasing number of pupils.

Meanwhile, efforts were being made to provide higher education in the town. A Mechanics' Institute was founded in 1834 and in 1855 its own building was opened. Here, and at the Church Institute, evening classes were held in a variety of subjects. By the end of the century Higher Grade Schools had been set up by the Wesleyans and the School Board. In 1909 a Technical School, School of Art and Girls' High School were opened in a new building on Ormerod Road.

After the Education Act of 1902, a committee of the Borough Council took over from the School Board. It was to be responsible for the implementation of many changes, such as the provision of secondary education for all after the 1944 Education Act, until it was superseded by the Lancashire Education Committee in the local government reorganisation of 1974.

The 19th century also saw the growth of professional entertainment in Burnley. Before this there is little evidence of how the townsfolk spent what little leisure time they had, but in 1751 local J.P.s had banned 'leaping, football, quoits, bowls, hunting, tippling in ale houses, swearing and cursing' on Sundays. Music had always played a part in religious life, and some of the earliest known performances were those of Handel's *Messiah* and *Acis and Galatea* at St Peter's church in 1778, which were noted in the diary of Elizabeth Shackleton of Alkincoates, Colne. Throughout the 19th century, many musical organisations were founded and there were frequent performances of oratorios and other vocal and orchestral works.

The earliest known theatre in the town was in 1798 on Bridge Street, where *The School for Scandal* was performed for one night. In 1814 plays were being presented in a room at the *Hall Inn* and from then onwards many buildings were used for performances, until purpose-built theatres were erected, such as the wooden Gaiety Theatre, or 'Blood Tub' (so-called because melodramas were performed there), which opened in 1880. The Victoria Theatre followed six years later, followed by the Empire Music Hall (1894) and the Palace Hippodrome (1907). In 1896 the Empire presented the first 'animated pictures' to be seen in Burnley and the cinematograph quickly became very popular, with many cinemas being built or converted from other buildings during the early years of the 20th century.

Sport was another important leisure activity, and in the early 19th century foot races, knurr and spell, stone bowling and horse racing were all popular. In 1828 a cricket team was formed which was later to become Burnley Cricket Club, and from 1860 there was another cricket club at Lowerhouse. In the 1880s football became very popular and the Burnley club, which was one of the founder members of the English Football League, came into being. Since then it has been responsible more than anything else for making Burnley known throughout the country.

During the last quarter of the century the town was provided with extensive parks and open spaces where the inhabitants could enjoy the fresh air. These included Scott and Queens Parks and several recreation grounds. In 1902 Towneley Hall and its grounds were acquired for use as a museum and art gallery, and later Ightenhill Park and Thompson Park were opened.

Burnley reached the height of its prosperity in the early years of the 20th century, since when there have been many developments, most, but not all, for the better. The traditional cotton-weaving industry has all but disappeared, and coal mining has ceased completely. In the 1930s, the town council realised that new industries would have to be attracted to the town and a Development Committee was set up. This met with some success and, particularly since the Second World War, diversification of industry within the town has continued, with many national companies setting up factories on new industrial estates.

In 1974, under local government reorganisation, the Borough was expanded to include some surrounding areas such as Padiham, which had been a separate town with its own identity and history; but at the same time Burnley lost control of many local services, such as education, libraries, the police and fire services, to Lancashire County Council.

In recent years the face of the town has almost completely changed. Slum housing has been replaced by modern estates, and smoke control has brought clean air so that it is now possible to see the surrounding hills. Use of the railway has declined and a motorway now cuts through the town; the centre has been pedestrianised and most of the family-owned shops have been replaced by multiple-stores and supermarkets. The photographs in this book illustrate many of these changes, and often depict a way of life which has now gone for ever.

Before Burnley

1. Bronze-Age burial circle at Mosely Height. This is one of a number of prehistoric burial places to be found on the moors to the east of Burnley. Many were dug up in the 19th century, but the one at Mosely Height near Mereclough received a more scientific excavation in 1950.

2. Excavation at Mosely Height, 1950. The excavation was directed by Walter Bennett, seen in the centre of the photograph. He was formerly history master at Burnley Grammar School and author of the four volume *History of Burnley*. Funerary urns and other artifacts from the site are now in Towneley Hall Museum.

3. The market cross. Although often referred to as the Paulinus Cross, there can be little doubt that this is really the market cross erected near to St Peter's church in 1295 at a cost of 9s. 1d. In 1617 a new market cross was put up and the old one was re-erected at the side of Godly Lane near the present Ormerod Road, where this photograph was taken, before it was moved in 1880 to its present site in the garden next to the Old Grammar School.

4. The Market Place in the 1830s, from a drawing by the Rev. S. J. Allen, headmaster of the Grammar School between 1834 and 1838. This area near to the church was known as 'Top o' th' Town'. In the centre are cottages which formed part of a market house built in the early 17th century. Next to them is the 'new' market cross, stocks, and the end of the *Old Sparrow Hawk Inn*. To the left can be seen the bridge over the river Brun and, in the distance, Bank Hall.

5.   St Peter's church in the mid-19th century. Although the church had a medieval foundation, the building here dates largely from the Tudor period, with the south aisle having been rebuilt in 1789. It is shown before the roof was raised and a clerestory added in 1854. In the foreground are the base of the market cross and stocks.

6.   Shorey Bank in *c*.1880. This drawing shows the buildings on the banks of the river Brun, with St Peter's church and the bridge which had been rebuilt in 1736. The houses on the right are the back of Dawson Square, and on the left is Shorey Street.

7.   Shorey Well. This well on the banks of the Brun was one of the town's main sources of drinking water until the 19th century. The well was approached along Shorey Street or by stepping stones across the river from Dawson Square. The well head can still be seen in the Grammar School garden.

8.   Burnley from Springhill in 1854. South Parade—now part of Manchester Road—leads into the town centre. In the distance is the tower of St Peter's church and on the left the railway viaduct opened in 1848. In the right-hand corner can be seen the roof of Thorneybank station and part of the goods yard, now the site of a D.I.Y. warehouse, although the stone gateposts still remain. Smoking chimneys sprout throughout the town, but sheep still graze within a quarter of a mile of the centre.

9.   The Market Place in 1854. By the middle of the 19th century the centre of the town had shifted from St Peter's to the junction of St James' Street and Manchester Road—known then as Market Street—shown here running to the left in front of the *Bull Inn*. At the very left is the *Swan Inn*, which still remains today, almost unaltered. In the centre is the Gawmless, a gas lamp first erected in 1823 and given its name because it stood in the middle of the road.

10. St James' Street, *c.*1900. Much remained unchanged, but the *Bull Inn* had become the *Bull Hotel*, and a more splendid Gawmless lit by electricity had been put up in 1893. The *Bull Hotel* was demolished in 1932 and replaced by the Burton's buildings.

11. St James' Street, *c.*1910. Almost all the buildings in this photograph were demolished in the 1960s. St James' Hall on the left still remains but its tower and clock have been taken down.

12. St James' Street in the 1890s. Munn's Corner was named after Robert Munn, chemist, and the town's registrar of births, marriages and deaths, whose shop can be seen on the left. Opposite is the *Clock Face Inn*. In the centre is the *Boot Inn* at the corner of Parker Lane, and next to it the tall gable of a row of shops built in 1876, which still survives today.

13. St James' Street, *c*.1930. This photograph shows a view similar to the previous scene after Munn's Corner had been demolished and the road widened in the early 1900s.

14. The bottom of Sandygate, which was one of the main thoroughfares out of the town before the Westgate turnpike road was built in the 1750s. The row of houses in the centre was known as Pencilling Shop Brow, as it was where block-printed calico was 'pencilled' to fill in the gaps in the pattern between the blocks. On the right is the *Plane Tree Inn*.

15. The west end of Church Street, *c.*1936. The unemployed service centre was opened in 1932; next to it is the site of Grimshaw's Keirby Brewery, where the *Friendly Hotel* is today. In the distance can be seen a Lancashire boiler on the site of Rishton Mill which had recently been demolished to make way for the Odeon cinema, opened in 1937.

16. Church Street, *c*1936. The first turning on the left, by the corner shop, was called Rake Foot. It led down to a tanyard by the river Brun in the 19th century.

17.   Manchester Road, *c*. 1905. The trams at that time went up the road only as far as a point just above the *Rose and Crown Inn*. The tracks were extended in December 1910 to a point which came to be called the Summit, though of course it is not actually at the top of Manchester Road.

18.   Manchester Road, showing the Town Hall and Mechanics' Institute. The Town Hall was opened on 27 October 1888; the architects were Holtom and Fox of Dewsbury who had won a competition to design the building. The Mechanics' Institute of 1855 is considered the better building architecturally, but might not have been so if the plans for the Town Hall had not been modified in the interest of economy.

19. Hammerton Street corner, Manchester Road, *c.*1905. Note the iron bollards to stop traffic from cutting round across the 'flags'; they feature in other pictures in this book, but not many remain in Burnley now. The cart is a 'flat', typically used by coalmen. The shops behind the street-lamp were demolished *c.*1987.

20. Manchester Road, near Nelson Square. These houses still stand, just above the canal bridge. Note the remarkable pram and the woman in clogs and shawl.

21. Hargreaves Street, not long before the building of the post office in 1905. The foundation stone of the Co-operative Society premises facing on to the street was laid by Thomas Hughes, author of *Tom Brown's Schooldays*, on 12 December 1885, the 25th anniversary of the opening of the first store at the junction of Hammerton Street and Cow Lane.

22. Yorkshire Street, from the canal aqueduct, looking towards Turf Moor football field, a section once well-known as Eastgate. On the right is St Mary's R.C. church. The sunblinds over the shops were once a common feature and most local ones were made by the firm of Arthur Whipp, Bridge Street.

23.   Burnley market hall. This drawing of 1866 shows the design by the architect, James Green, to replace a building erected by the Burnley Market Company. The new market hall was opened in 1870, although the tower was never built. The market hall was demolished, with some difficulty, in June 1966, during the redevelopment of the town centre.

24.   The market hall interior decorated for some special occasion—perhaps Queen Victoria's Diamond Jubilee in 1897.

25. The Market Place, *c.*1900. Burnley's market dates back to a charter of 1294, and was originally held near to St Peter's church. In the early 19th century it moved to the bottom of Manchester Road, and then in the 1850s to the area round the market hall. This photograph shows some of the stalls surrounding the market hall of 1870.

26. Webster's butcher's, Church Street, Padiham. The old shop was demolished shortly after the building behind it was completed in 1898. The display of meat hanging outside would not meet with today's public health regulations.

27. Hepworth's tailor's, *c*.1890. Joseph Hepworth and Son of Leeds occupied these premises on St James' Street for only a few years around 1890; an example of a non-Burnley based firm setting up a shop in the town. Next door is the *Thorn Hotel*, one of Burnley's best-known inns. It had its origins in Thorn Farm which became a tavern in the 18th century. John Wesley preached outside the *Thorn* in 1786.

28.   Milk-float at Padiham. Until well after the Second World War almost all your daily needs were met by either the corner shop or by delivery to the door. Milk-floats like this one were a part of every morning in the streets; in fact there were two deliveries per day up to *c*.1940.

29. Metcalfe's grocer's in the 1920s. A typical grocer's shop before the days of the self-service supermarket, with biscuits displayed in tins, and goods stacked high on the counter and shelves. Metcalfe Bros. establisehd their business on St James' Street in the 1890s, and by the date of this photograph had branches in Nelson, Padiham, Todmorden, St Annes and Oldham.

30. The Empire Buildings. An architect's drawing of seven shops on St James' Street erected by the corporation and opened in 1927. The names of the shops are fictitious, and the name of the block—here called Victoria Buildings—was changed in reality to Empire Buildings. They still stand.

31.   Sagar Hill Farm, Higham in 1905, occupied by the Thornber family. The girl worked as a weaver at Fir Trees mill. Her brother, Stephen, ran a carrier's business with a horse called Charlie. The calf is a shorthorn, a breed superseded by Ayrshires and Friesians and then by continental cattle. The dog is an all-purpose farm dog rather than the more refined border collie that would be usual nowadays.

32.   Muck-spreading at Ightenhill. Something we shall never see again, though it was an annual farming practice from earliest times until the end of the horse era in the 1940s and '50s. Tractors began to take over locally from *c*.1922.

33. Weavers' cottages at Lanebottom. These are typical of the many hand-loom weavers' cottages built in the late 18th century. The work was carried out in a loom-shop, usually on an upper floor with large windows to provide the light necessary for fine work. At Hill Factory, the three-storey building towards the right, the top floor, over several cottages, housed in the region of twenty looms.

34. Plan showing mills, 1742. This plan, made during the course of a law-suit, shows the earliest known factories in Burnley. They were a dye-house, a cloth mill and a fulling mill built between 1736 and 1741 by John and Henry Halstead on the banks of the river Calder. Bridge End House, the home of Henry Halstead, was later owned by members of the Peel family, and in the 19th century became the *Calder Vale Inn*.

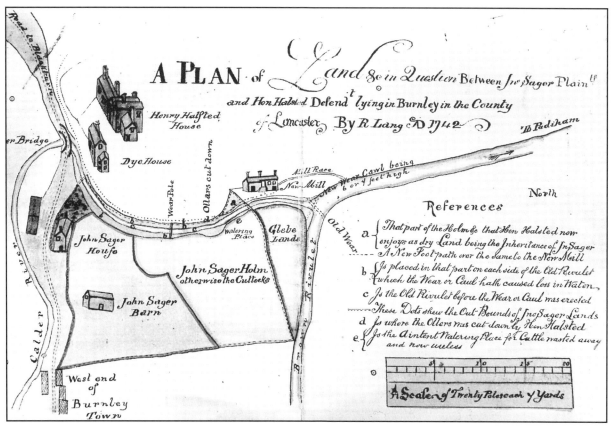

35.   Lowerhouse printworks. This picture, believed to have been painted in about 1830, shows the factory begun by the Peel family and Richard Yates in 1795, which was one of Burnley's earliest industrial sites. Originally a spinning mill, it was sold to the Dugdale family in 1813, who, a few years later, began to print as well as manufacture calicoes. In 1836, they built a large new mill on a site just off the left edge of the picture. Near to the works can be seen a terrace of workers' houses known as Long Row (now Bear Street), and, in the factory itself, a large house which was the home of the owners.

36.   Industrial Burnley, *c.*1910. This area of Burnley, now known as the Weavers' Triangle, was at the heart of the town's textile industry. Here, the factories cluster along the banks of the Leeds and Liverpool Canal in the angle between Westgate to the left and Trafalgar Street to the right. Most of them date from after 1842 when mills were allowed to take water from the canal to use in their boilers. Many of the factories are still there, but none produces cotton, and of the forest of chimneys only a handful remains.

37.   Clock Tower Mill was built as a spinning mill in the 1840s by George Slater, one of Burnley's leading industrialists. A few years later a weaving shed was added and then in 1863, during rebuilding after a fire, the clock tower which gave it its name was erected. Later in the century the mill was taken over by the cotton-waste merchants John Watts. Unfortunately, Burnley lost one of its best industrial monuments in April 1987, when part of the mill was destroyed by fire, and the clock tower had to be demolished as it was unsafe.

38.   Weaving at Trafalgar Shed, a scene typical of most Burnley factories at the turn of the century. The looms stood in long rows on the stone floor, driven by belts from the shafting above. The shed was lit from the north-light roof which gave plenty of illumination but avoided direct rays from the sun in an attempt to maintain the humidity necessary to prevent the yarn from breaking.

39.   Loading cloth at Trafalgar Shed. By the end of the 19th century almost all Burnley mills were concentrating on weaving, mainly producing the plain calico known as 'Burnley printers'. Most was exported, and it was said that the cloth woven before breakfast was for the home market, while that produced afterwards went abroad.

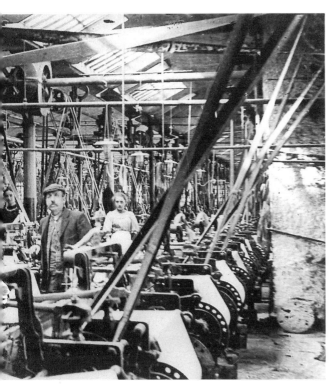

40. Electrically driven looms at Heasandford
Shed, 1904. These were the first looms in the town
to be powered by individual electric motors, rather
than shafting driven by a steam engine.

41.   Byerden Mill after a fire, 1905. Fire was always a big hazard in cotton mills. Oil soaked floors and inflammable cotton waste meant that a carelessly dropped match or even a spark from the machinery could lead to disaster. There were few factories in the town that did not suffer in this way at some time. Here, in spite of the efforts of the fire brigade and the availability of abundant water in the canal, most of the mill was destroyed.

42. Steam Engine at Harle Syke Mill. This is typical of the engines that drove the machinery in the cotton mills. It was made at Burnley Ironworks and installed in the factory in 1904. Today it can be seen, in working order, in the Science Museum in London.

43. Aerial view of industrial Burnley, *c.*1930. This is another photograph of the area now known as the Weavers' Triangle. At the bottom right is Clock Tower Mill, and Sandygate Bridge over the canal. Next to it is Slater Terrace, an unusual terrace of 11 houses over a canal-side warehouse. The mills crowd in on the canal and the north-light roofs of the weaving sheds can be clearly seen. Close to the factories are the rows of houses where the workers lived.

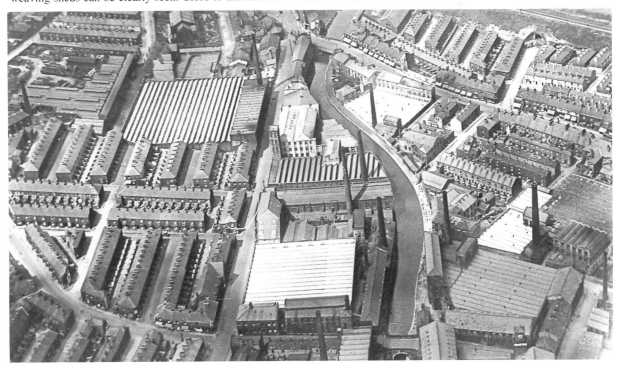

44.   Burnley Ironworks in 1921. This foundry, begun in 1793 by the Marsland family, was one
of the largest in the town. The photograph shows the flywheel of a steam engine being tested,
before being exported to a mill in Bombay.

45.   Bank Top Pit, Curzon Street, also known as Bankhouse Pit and Parsonage Colliery, was worked out in 1864;
therefore this must be one of the earliest Burnley photographs that we have. It was one of several small collieries which
were to be found near to the centre of the town in the mid-19th century. Just beyond the pit is the bridge carrying the
railway over Curzon Street, and on the right is the *Prince Albert Inn*. Notice the arched doorway which led to a yard and
stables. This was still *in situ* when the inn was demolished in January 1987.

46.   The pit top at Bank Hall Pit, a big colliery by local standards which employed about a thousand men in its heyday. It closed in 1971 and the site was transformed into parkland.

47. Coal strike at Cheapside Pit, 1921. Men, women and children had to collect fuel for use at home from the tip at Cheapside, between Burnley and Padiham.

48. Hapton Valley Pit Disaster. On 22 March 1962, 16 men were killed and 25 injured at Hapton Valley by an underground explosion in Burnley's worst-ever mining disaster. They have a memorial at the cemetery, and were especially in mind when the memorial to all Burnley miners of the past was dedicated at Bank Hall in September 1990.

49.   Bridge End Brewery, c.1880. This brewery on Westgate, owned by the Massey family, produced what was probably Burnley's best known beer. Edward Stocks Massey, who died in 1909, left about £120,000 to Burnley Corporation for the advancement of education, music, art and science.

50.   Platers and Stampers, 1937. In the 1930s, the decline of Burnley's traditional industries led the town council to set up a Development Committee to attract new firms to the town. In 1937 they used the rates to help finance the building of the factory, seen here in the course of construction, although at the time it was not legal to do so. Today the works is owned by Prestige Ltd.

51. Knocker-up. You had to be up early if you worked at the mill or the pit. The knocker-up was still in some demand even after cheap alarm-clocks became available, and it was into the 1970s before the last one, Robinson Rainey, retired completely.

Somewhere to Live

52. Wapping. The development of industry necessitated the provision of homes for the rapidly increasing number of workers in the town. By the mid-19th century the district between St James' Street, Bridge Street and the river Brun was a warren of narrow streets known as Wapping. Here small industrial buildings like the warehouse, seen here, adjoined some of the poorest slums.

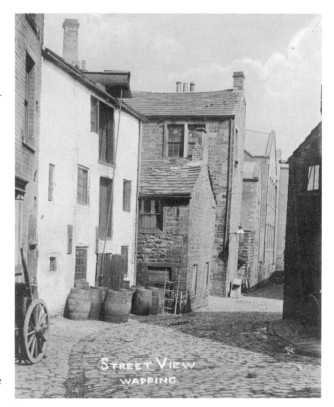

53. Mount Pleasant Court in the 1930s—a far from pleasant place to live. Sometimes more than one family lived in each of the back-to-back houses. Sanitation was provided by the privies in the centre of the picture, but in spite of the dismal conditions one lady is keen to keep the street clean.

54.   Croft Street in 1936. Many of the houses were in the centre of the town and these on Croft Street, opposite where the bus station is today, look substantial. However, a passage in the centre leads to Croft Court on the other side, and over-crowding and lack of basic amenities meant the homes were far below the standard expected today. The building on the right of the passage was used as a common lodging house.

55.   Kitchen at Hill Top. This photograph was taken after the house had been abandoned prior to demolition in the 1930s. The room has a typical iron fire range with oven and boiler, which would usually have been kept sparklingly clean. Note the stone sink and mangle; often the family lived, cooked, ate and did the washing in just the one room.

56.   Healey Wood. Later in the 19th century, rather better housing began to be provided. Row upon row of terraces, like the ones seen here, were built, usually running downhill to assist with the drainage. Each had its own running water and outside toilet, but they lacked gardens and were often very near to the place of work.

57.   Causeway End, *c.*1890—middle-class suburbia, Todmorden Road. Here lived the Sutcliffes, Butterworths, Thompsons and Scotts—the people who ran the town and on the whole were generous with donations and legacies. The gate to the footpath called the Rabbit Walks can be seen. There was great controversy here in 1857-9, when Col. Towneley tried to deny the public's right of access to it.

58.   The *Old Sparrow Hawk Inn*, 1890. There has been a tavern on this site since the Middle Ages, taking its name, no doubt, from the sparrow hawk which was the crest of the Towneley family. This photograph was taken at a furniture sale in 1890 shortly before the inn was demolished. Part of the new building, which replaced it, can be seen in the course of construction on the right.

59.   The *Talbot Inn, c.*1886. This tavern which stood close to the *Old Sparrow Hawk,* was originally known as the *Parker Arms*. The photograph was taken after the road was widened by demolishing the old market house and cottages which stood immediately in front of the inn. To the left is the end of Shorey Street and then the bridge over the river Brun, with Dawson Square on the far side.

60. The *Boot Inn*, *White Lion* and *Clock Face*. These three taverns line one side of St James's Street. The first two survive in more modern buildings, although the *Boot* is now *Yates Wine Lodge*. The *Clock Face*, now replaced by shops, was once owned by William Slater, father of George who built Clock Tower Mill.

61. The *Bull Hotel*, 1904. Originally a farmhouse, the *Bull* was one of the town's most important inns in the 19th century and a centre of its social activity. Its best known landlord was Richard Rothwell, Burnley's last stage-coach driver, who had operated from the tavern. The tram on the left was one of the first to operate on the route from Manchester Road to Towneley.

62. The *Sun Inn*, Bridge Street, was the venue for meetings of the Vestry Committee in the early years of the 19th century, when Miles Veevers was the landlord. It was closed in 1925 and converted into Hudson's leather shop. To the right of the inn is one of Burnley's oldest textile mills, and next to that Gorman's school of arms and gymnasium.

63. *Cronkshaw's Commercial Hotel* on Grimshaw Street closed as such in April 1925. It had traditionally been the headquarters of the local Liberals, and was specially renowned for its New Year dinners. The property which belonged to a daughter of Adam and Mrs. Dugdale of Rosehill House, has been converted into offices, but is still recognisable as being once residential.

64. The *Nelson Inn*, Trafalgar Street, *c.*1905. This inn has survived almost unchanged. The view along the street is still much the same, but it is now one of the town's busiest thoroughfares; no-one would gather in the road to have a photograph taken today.

65. The *Black Bull Inn*, Lanehead in the early 1900s with the newly-opened Marsden Hospital in the background. It is interesting to speculate as to who might have owned the rather stylish carriage—possibly Rhoda Holden who lived at Reedley House, only half a mile away.

66. St Peter's church, *c.*1900. The porch had been added in
1889, but the clergy vestry was not added until 1903-4.
(See also plate 5.)

67.   St Peter's church interior, *c.*1900. At first glance the scene
looks much as it did before the recent alterations (1988-92), but
the lectern and pulpit are positioned differently, and the west and
south galleries are still *in situ*. These were removed in 1903-4;
the picture therefore dates from some little time before.

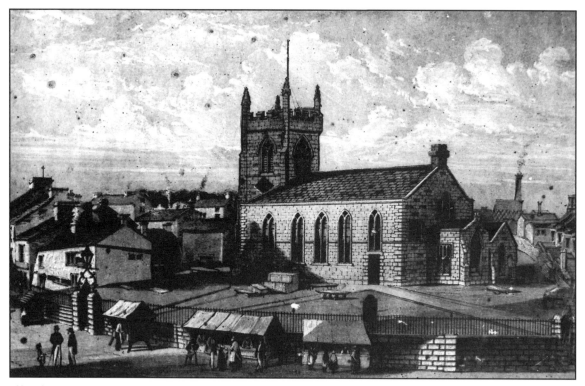

68.   St Leonard's church, Padiham, with market stalls around it in a drawing from *c*.1850. The church was re-built as we see it here in 1766, and again re-built in 1869.

69.   St John the Baptist's church, Gannow Lane, *c*.1900. The church was opened in 1880 and demolished in 1984. The area around Woodbine farm on the left was still undeveloped.

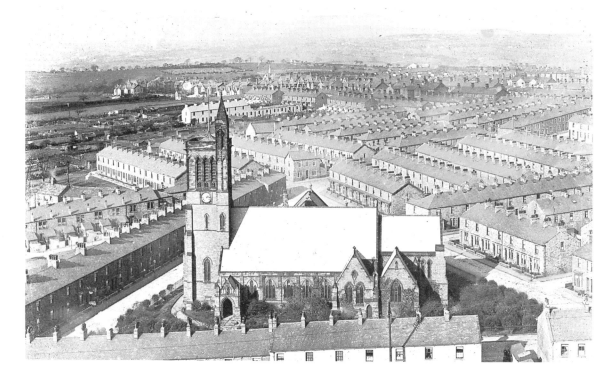

70. St Matthew's church, *c*.1890, with the line of old Blind Lane coming down across the field behind the cottages we knew as Treacle Row. These were demolished in December 1955. At one time officially Further Row, they became Treacle Row to everybody after another row of that name lower down Coal Clough Lane was demolished at about the turn of the century. The church was badly damaged by fire on Christmas Day 1927 and had to be largely rebuilt.

71. St Mary's Roman Catholic church. A drawing of the proposed church, opened on 2 August 1849, but without the intended spire, which was never built because of lack of funds. It replaced an earlier building called the Burnley Wood chapel, which stood alongside Todmorden Road where Tarleton Avenue is now.

72.　The first Haggate Baptist chapel, built in 1767 and 'mother' to others not only in Briercliffe, but in Burnley, Brierfield and Nelson.

73.　Keighley Green chapel was the first Methodist place of worship in Burnley (1788-1840), the town's court and police station (1851-1888) and the Burnley Lads' Club headquarters (1907-1947). It was demolished in 1976. In the middle period, the court room doubled as a concert hall when not required by the magistrates and police.

74. Brunswick chapel, Manchester Road opened in 1869. The nationally-renowned novelists Joseph and Silas Hocking were ministers here in the chapel's heyday. Silas' most successful book *Her Benny*—still in print—was written in Burnley, at the manse on Albion Terrace.

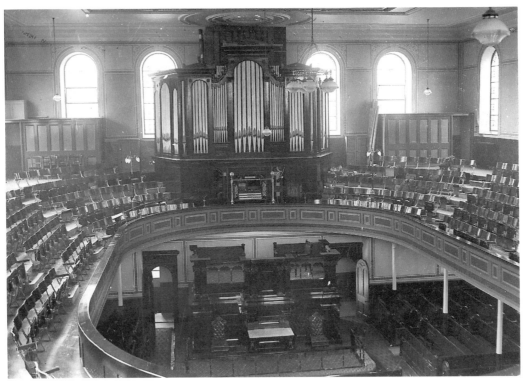

75. Wesley chapel, Hargreaves Street. The interior of a Nonconformist chapel usually differed from that of a traditional church, as we see from this photograph taken *c*.1900. The chapel was built in 1840 as a development from Keighley Green. It was demolished in 1965 and the present Central Methodist church was built on the site.

76. Fulledge chapel, Todmorden Road, closed as a place of worship in 1959 and was eventually demolished in 1992, after it had stood as a ruin since a fire in September 1985. It was tremendously influential in its day. There was an elementary school attached, which in about 1880 had over 1,000 scholars and was the largest of its kind in England. The new Todmorden Road School took its older pupils in 1908, but it went on as an infant school until 1942.

77.   Whitsun Walks in Padiham, 1914, by which time they had been established for over fifty years. The district of Burnley as a whole is weak on traditions—in fact it is difficult to think of any apart from this which is still maintained as an annual event.

78.   The demolition of Brunswick chapel, January 1963, shortly to be followed by that of St Paul's church in the background—emphasising the decline in organised religion. St Paul's, consecrated in 1853, was vacated as unsafe in May 1961.

79.   The Council Chamber, 1930. The photograph shows the council chamber much as it must have appeared when the building was new in 1888. Today the furnishings have been replaced and the portraits removed, but the decorative ceiling has been retained and restored.

80.   The police force is shown here in 1893 outside the police station which, together with the magistrates' court, formed part of the Town Hall from 1888 until 1955 when they moved to the new building on Parker Lane.

81.   The fire brigade demonstrates a new fire escape *c*.1890. It looks primitive, but was no doubt a valuable addition to the fire-fighting equipment. In 1861 the senior sergeant replied to criticism of his brigade's performance by pointing out that most of his men were volunteers with other jobs, and had to run to the fire when the alarm sounded, often arriving in a state of exhaustion.

FIRE ENGINE STATION

82. *(above left)* The fire station, Manchester Road, in 1913, decorated for the visit of George V to the town. The building was erected in 1881, replacing an earlier one on the same site. It was demolished after the present fire station on Belvedere Road was opened in 1965.

83. *(left)* The fire brigade, *c.*1922, when it was changing over from using horses to motorised vehicles. The firemen lived on Hammerton Street, River Street and Nelson Square, not far from the fire station on Manchester Road.

84. *(above)* Wood End Sewage Works in 1931, after some modernisation. This is not an exciting picture but important because Walter Bennett in his *History of Burnley* identifies the establishment of an efficient sewerage system as the main reason for improvement in the town's health record after about 1875.

85.   Victoria Hospital. This drawing commemorates the opening of the hospital by Prince Albert Victor on 13 October 1886. It was built by public subscription at a cost of £21,578, on ground given by the Rev. William Thursby.

86.   A ward at the Victoria Hospital. This is one of two circular wards, named the Butterworth and Thursby wards after two of the hospital's benefactors.

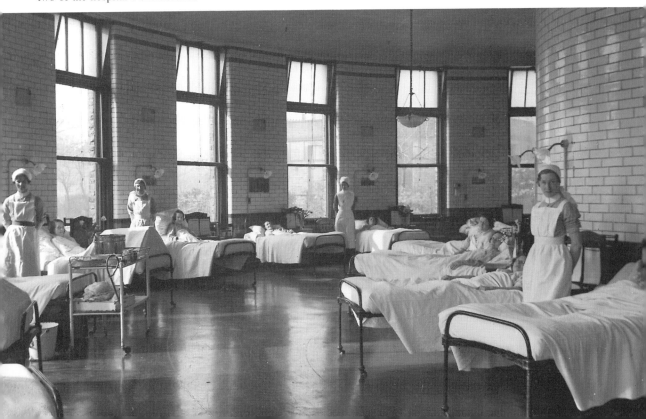

87.   Primrose Bank Workhouse and Infirmary, c.1900. On the left is the infirmary building opened as part of the workhouse in 1895. The workhouse itself was opened in 1877 and can be seen in the distance. In the 1930s the infirmary became the Municipal Hospital and both buildings are now part of Burnley General Hospital.

88.   The workhouse interior c.1900. This photograph shows the sewing room at the workhouse. When the building opened in 1877 it could accommodate 350 paupers. Many were aged and infirm, but those who were able-bodied were set to work.

89.   Burnley Grammar School boys in 1865, with their headmaster, Dr. Butler, and his deputy, Thomas Turner Wilkinson (on the left). Mr. Wilkinson was a very sound historian: his accounts of St Peter's church (1856) and of the Grammar School (1870) are still essential for serious study of those subjects.

90. The Old Grammar School, Bank Parade—one of several fine builings in Burnley designed by the local architect Angelo Waddington. It replaced an older building nearby in 1873-4 and continued in use as the town's grammar school until new premises across the town at Habergham were opened in August 1959. Though threatened by demolition in the 1980s, it is still in educational use and is well maintained.

91. Habergham School. This National School was founded in 1832 at the instigation of Janet Shuttleworth, who was later to marry James Philips Kay, one of the country's leading educationalists, who took the name Kay-Shuttleworth. The school closed in 1983, and has now been demolished, apart from the school-house in the centre, which bears the initials J.S. and the date 1840.

92.   Children at St John's school, Worsthorne, 1905. The photograph shows a group of pupils taking part in a scene from Shakespeare's *Merchant of Venice*.

93.   A domestic science class at Heasandford Senior Girls' School shortly after it opened on 7 September 1937. The school became a technical high school in July 1945 and closed in that capacity at the end of the summer term in 1956.

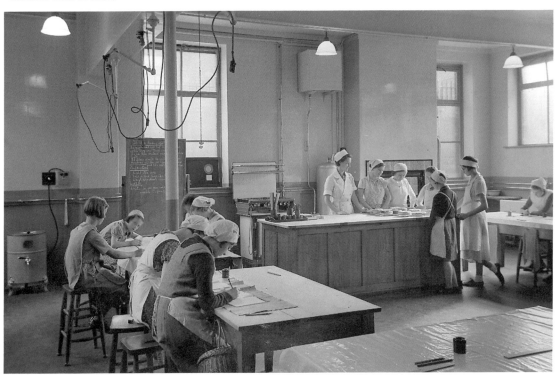

94.   Burnley Mechanics' Institute depicted in a drawing by its architect James Green. Opened in July 1855, it soon became Burnley's social and academic centre, unrivalled until technical education became available elsewhere and public libraries took on other aspects of its work. Its furnishings and equipment were sold in August 1959. The building fell into disrepair and only just escaped demolition, but has now been restored. It opened as an arts centre in 1986.

95.   Art class at Burnley Mechanics', early this century. Art classes were held in the Mechanics' as early as 1858, but not until October 1880 was there a 'self-contained' art school there. It was moved to a new wing of the building in October 1888, remaining there until transferred to Ormerod Road in 1909.

96.   An engineering class at the Technical Institute on Ormerod Road, *c.*1937. The Institute was opened in September 1909, incorporating the School of Art and Burnley Girls' High School (which was there until 1954). We know it now as Burnley College.

97.   Building the central library, opened in July 1930. Quite a comprehensive library service had developed in Burnley by that date, but it was too fragmented to be at all satisfactory. The new building became the hub of a more efficient system and was soon the centre of Burnley's cultural life.

98.   The children's department at the central library in 1930, in what later became the lecture hall. The children were moved to a lighter room downstairs in April 1937 because the one in the picture was 'too gloomy'.

99.   Toll bar and canal aqueduct, *c.*1820. This drawing shows the toll bar at Eastgate—part of Yorkshire Street—on the turnpike road to Todmorden. In the distance is the aqueduct, referred to locally as the Culvert, in the embankment carrying the Leeds and Liverpool Canal.

100.   The Culvert, *c.*1920. Originally, there was only the main opening, but in 1896-7 two additional 'gimlet holes' were bored for the convenience of pedestrians.

101.   Rebuilding the Culvert. In 1925-6 the entire aqueduct was replaced with a new one which carried the water in a metal channel. During the work, the canal was diverted into a temporary channel, as can be seen here. The stretch of canal on the embankment, known as the 'straight mile', is regarded as one of the seven wonders of the British canal system.

102.   The new Culvert in 1925, showing the old one underneath which, when removed, more than doubled the width of the roadway.

103.   Manchester Road Wharf, c.1900. There has been a wharf here since this section of the canal was opened in 1801. The stone warehouse with the cranes dates from this time, while the other warehouses with the canopies were added later in the 19th century. The wharf is a hive of activity, with a variety of goods being unloaded, while other boats wait on the opposite side of the canal.

104.   Log transporter at Finsley Gate, *c*.1900. The huge piece of timber, too long to carry on a boat, is being brought by road to one of the most important maintenance yards on the Leeds and Liverpool Canal, to be cut up and used for repairs, possibly of lock gates or boats.

105.   Brig Steps at Healey Wood. As Burnley grew, the canal was to prove something of a barrier to expansion. This photograph shows one of several foot-bridges which were built to enable people to cross the canal without having to make a detour via one of the road bridges.

106. Barges at Reedley brickworks. Water transport was particularly suitable for heavy goods such as building materials, and industrial sites were often located close to the canal.

107.   Bank Top station, *c.*1860. This photograph shows the station which was opened in December 1848. The platforms are very low and there is just a single station building. On the left can be seen the goods warehouse and several wagons.

108.   Bank Top station in the 20th century. The station has been extended, canopies added and a second building erected on the down line to Colne. The name was changed to Burnley Central in 1944, and eventually the station was completely rebuilt, leaving only a small building served by a single-track line.

Bank Top Station, Burnley.

109. Viaduct collapse, 1908. The railway was carried across the valley on a massive viaduct. On 4 July 1908 Greenhalgh's dyeworks collapsed, affecting the viaduct's foundations, and causing cracks to appear and part of the parapet to dislodge. The line had to be closed to enable repairs to take place, and the 'temporary' wooden parapet can still be seen today.

110.   Rosegrove station was originally further down the line towards Burnley than the present station, as can be seen in this photograph, and was reached by a footpath from Rosegrove Lane. Also at Rosegrove was a large goods marshalling yard, and an engine shed which was one of the last three in Britain to house steam locomotives when it closed in 1968.

111.   James Redford and *Mazzeppa* at Manchester Road station. A personality in his day, he was not only a well-known and respected engine-driver, but also a pioneer of photography in Burnley. His home was on Sackville Street, adjacent to the station, and still stands. He died, aged 68, in November 1887.

112.   Carters outside Queen's Park, early 1900s—possibly photographed because this was their last load before going over to motor transport. The leather aprons worn by the carter and his mate were a mark of their trade.

113.   Halstead's shoeing forge on Yorkshire Street, founded in 1830 and maintained successively by three generations of the family. The picture was taken in October 1929 when the business was removing to new premises on Blakey Street.

114.   Steam tram, *c*.1888. These were introduced to Burnley in 1881 but were never a success; more than once they had to be temporarily replaced by horse-drawn trams on some local routes. Electric trams superseded them from December 1901.

115.   Padiham: awaiting the arrival of the first electric tram, 4 January 1902. There had been steam trams before that, but none at all during the previous six months whilst the new lines were being laid. In the words of a *Burnley Express* reporter, 'All Padiham seemed to turn out; there were hundreds in the streets and scores were peeping from all available windows'.

116.   The last tram from Harle Syke to Rosegrove, superseded on that route by the bus service in 4 April 1932.

117.   The Habergham, a private bus built by John Knape at the Bank Top works in Burnley for the Burnley Motor Pleasure Company, of which Mr. W. E. Cooke was the manager. It is pictured here outside Mitton church on its first trial run in June 1906.

118.   The first Burnley Corporation bus, 17 March 1924. Designed by the tramways department, it resembled a tram in that the seats ran lengthwise not across. As in the trams, parcels were carried, and workmen's discount tickets were available at certain times of the day. It ran from the cattle market to Abel Street.

119.   The bus station on the cattle market, *c.*1950. The grimy appearance of the buildings is very noticeable and those that survive look better now, thanks to stone-cleaning.

120.   Motor car *c.*1904. The first car to come through Burnley was seen at the end of November 1896. Dr. Mackenzie is credited with being the town's first car-owner, and the one in this picture was originally his, though when the photograph was taken it was registered to Peter Altham, one of the Altham's tea firm. The children may be his, but the man at the back remains unidentified.

121. Car smash, 1909. Mr. Henry Shaw of Blackburn was driving along Padiham Road in the early hours of 25 June, when his car 'dashed against a tramway pole in the middle of the road'. He and his companions were lucky to escape with only a few scratches.

MOTOR SMASH
CHEAPSIDE.
JUNE 25TH 1909

122. Widening the Mitre bridge, 1935; a leisurely scene comparable with what one would expect today. The contractors were Wimpey's, better known nowadays in connection with the development of private housing estates.

123. Monoplane at Turf Moor, October 1909, on exhibition at the Burnley athletic grounds near Brunshaw; it had been ordered from a London maker by Mr. W. E. Cooke, who commissioned the Habergham Bus three years previously. It never actually flew in Burnley; there were quarrels between those who had a financial interest in it, and it was quickly sold to a Bradford syndicate.

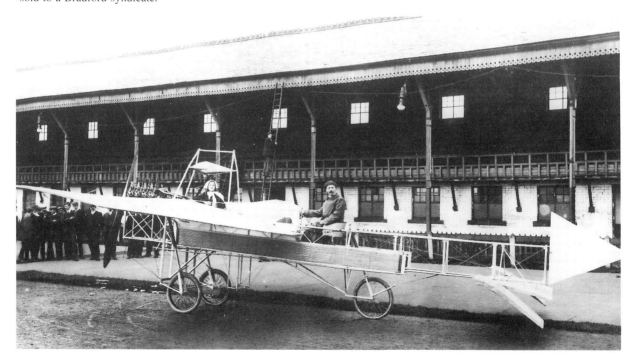

124.   Burnley Fair, 1908. The annual fair was originally for the sale of goods and animals, but eventually only the pleasure fair with its roundabouts, swings and booths remained. It was held early in July during the town's holiday week on the cattle market, where the magistrates' court and police station stand today.

125.   Burnley F.C. v. Sunderland in an F.A. Cup 4th round match at Turf Moor, 11 March 1914. Burnley won 2 - 1 with goals by Dick Lindley and Teddy Hodgson. Forty-nine thousand people were in attendance, breaking the previous ground record by more than ten thousand.

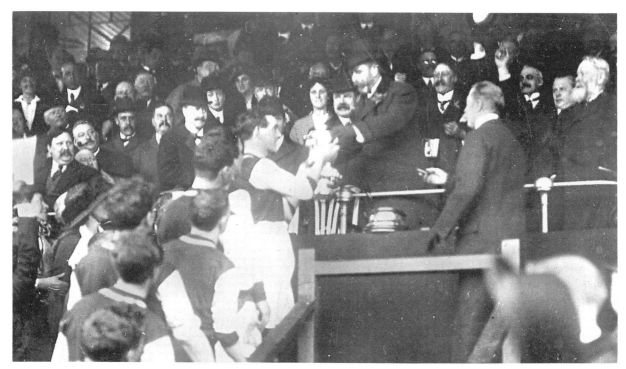

126.   George V presenting the F.A. Cup. On the big day, 25 April 1914, in the final held at Crystal Palace, Burnley beat Liverpool 1 - 0, Freeman the scorer. For the first time the cup was presented by the reigning monarch, who is seen here handing it to Burnley captain, Tommy Boyle.

127.   Burnley F.C. returning with the F.A. Cup, seen here outside Rosegrove station. So many people thronged the space outside the Town Hall that plans for a civic presentation had to be abandoned and the team travelled on to Turf Moor for celebrations there.

128. The Victoria Theatre opened in September 1886. In the early years of the Second World War, the Old Vic and Sadler's Wells companies from London made it their regional headquarters. It closed in March 1955 and was demolished at the end of that year. Shops now occupy the site.

129. The Palace Theatre, St James' Street was built in record time by Smith Brothers of Burnley. They signed the contract for it on 18 June 1907 and it was opened on 2 December in the same year. In its time it housed vaudeville, silent pictures and talkies, live theatre and bingo, and was demolished in April 1973.

130.   Burnley Operatic Society at the Palace Theatre, February 1922. A memorable performance of *Cavalleria Rusticana* by Burnley amateurs. The orchestra was conducted by Cecil Bateson and the producer was Lee Thistlethwaite.

131.   The Savoy Cinema in 1953; it opened as a 'picture theatre and café' in 1922 and was later the first in Burnley to screen talkies. It showed its last films in 1956 and was demolished in 1961 to be replaced by Martin's Bank.

132. The Mechanics' Institute ballroom, well remembered as the scene of music festivals and school prize-givings. Now re-designed as a theatre.

133. The Empress Ballroom, 1927. Roller-skating mania took hold of Burnley in 1909 and the Palace Skating Rink was opened, among others, to meet the sudden demand. The fashion soon faded and the rink was succeeded by the Pavilion Picture Palace, which in its turn gave way to the Empress Ballroom and Roller-Skating Rink, opened in December 1927. It burnt down in a spectacular fire on 13 November 1960.

134. Scott Park in its early days. The people are probably leaving after a band concert of the kind that once attracted literally thousands. Opened in August 1895, visitors were instructed to 'keep to the walks'. A bowling-green had been made by 1897, but there were no children's playgrounds before 1913 or tennis courts before 1925.

135.   The opening of Towneley Park, June 1902. The photograph shows the platform party outside the hall, which was opened to the public in the following year on 20 May.

136.   The opening of the Massey Music Pavilion, Towneley Park, in 1929. Burnley's weather was always against events there being a success and, after the pavilion was damaged by fire in August 1963, there was no serious opposition to its demolition.

137.   Work in progress on the site of Thompson Park, opened in July 1930. At a time of high unemployment, it was calculated to provide work for 50 men for just over a year, at a weekly wage of £2 15s. It was conceived as more recreational than the earlier parks; nevertheless, it was not until 1938 that the playground was open on Sundays, and then only in summer time.

138.   The Italian garden, Thompson Park. The park was paid for out of a legacy by J. W. Thompson, another of whose family, William Thompson, was later to finance the Thompson Centre. The Italian garden was something rather special, with its flower beds and formal pond, the latter now regrettably filled-in.

139. Jack Moore's monkey at Pendle Bottom Gardens in the early 1900s. 'Jack Moore's', the pleasure gardens at Holme End, were established in about 1840 and continued to the late 1960s. Special corporation buses ran there on Good Fridays in the 1930s, and record attendances were achieved in 1936. The Rogers family—related to the Moores by marriage—are still in residence but their business is now entirely horticultural.

EPPING STONES NR BURNLEY No 4
A GOOD FRIDAY SCENE

140.   The stepping stones across the Calder below Ightenhill were always a popular destination on fine weekends, especially at Easter, until the site lost some of its appeal when they were replaced by a bridge in 1928. This was destroyed by a flood in 1979 and the present bridge is a replacement set up in the following year.

141. Children's day out in July 1928. An outing to Whalley organised by the local committee of Pearson's Fresh-air Fund. Poverty was very obvious in Burnley until the 1940s. As late as 1937 a local charitable fund to provide clogs for poor children distributed 891 pairs during the year.

142. Altham's day trip to Blackpool. Abraham Altham was a local grocer and tea-merchant, who eventually owned 64 shops throughout Lancashire, Yorkshire and the Midlands. In 1874 he began to organise rail excursions to the seaside, selling tickets through his shops. Altham's Tours became a Lancashire institution and, although there are no longer any grocer's shops, Altham's Travel Services are still flourishing.

143.   Towneley Hall, seen here in 1808, had its origins in a medieval house dating from about 1400, but extensive rebuilding has meant that little of this remains. The Towneleys were the area's leading Roman Catholic family, being involved in many events of national importance. The hall and its extensive parklands were acquired by the town in 1902.

144. Interior of Towneley Hall, *c.*1900. This photograph shows the entrance hall as it was furnished in the days immediately prior to the sale of the building to Burnley Corporation.

145. Kettledrum, Derby winner in 1861. Col. Towneley put Burnley on the map with his horse, but Kettledrum was seldom, if ever, at Towneley; he lived most of his life at Whitewell in Bowland. He was sold to Sir T. Leonard for 550 guineas when Col. Towneley disposed of all his racing stock in 1870, and was exported to Hungary in 1872.

146.   Towneley cattle. As Kettledrum brought prestige to Col. Towneley on the turf, so did the Towneley cattle make a name for him in agricultural circles. Joseph Culshaw, who was in charge of them, lived at Castle Hill in his old age with his niece Caroline, seen here with her own painting of a few of the famous herd.

147.   Towneley gatehouses, Todmorden Road. The house on the left, nicknamed Handbridge Castle, was demolished in 1958. It was built in about 1797 and became the home of the Towneley's land agent Edward Lovat, an important figure in Burnley's history for all that he did to improve standards in local farming. He died in 1841, not long after building Tarleton House which stands not far away.

148.   Gawthorpe Hall in the early 19th century. The hall was built between 1600 and 1605 around a medieval pele tower. It was the home of the Shuttleworths, another of the area's great land-owning families. This drawing shows the building before it was remodelled by Sir Charles Barry in 1850 for Sir James Kay-Shuttleworth.

149.   Gawthorpe Hall with members of the Shuttleworth family. Ughtred, Sir James' eldest son and successor, was created a baron in 1902. One of his daughters, the Hon. Rachel Kay-Shuttleworth, amassed a large and important collection of textiles and embroidery, part of which is on display at the hall which was given to the National Trust in 1970.

BURNLEY'S V.C. AND YOUNG KITCHENER.

150. 'Young Kitchener' and Thomas Whitham, Jennie Jackson ('Young Kitchener') and Amy Foster ('Hielan Lassie') were two children who raised thousands of pounds locally for various aspects of the war effort, 1914-18. Here is Jennie with Worsthorne-born Pte. Thomas Whitham, V.C. He won his award by capturing a German machine-gun and its crew single-handed, thus saving many British lives and enabling the whole line to advance.

151. The town's war memorial at Towneley, dedicated on 12 December 1926. Some dissatisfaction arose in the 1950s and early 1960s because it was felt to be too far out from the town centre, and a new memorial by the library was therefore provided. It was unveiled in the autumn of 1966.

152. *(above)* The Home Guard on Standish Street. Enrolment for the Burnley Local Defence Volunteers began in May 1940 and ended with the Home Guard's standing-down in early December 1944.

153. *(below)* Making munitions, *c*.1943. There is not much to be said in favour of wars, but they did perhaps enhance the status of women by giving them greater job opportunities. Here are women making munitions at Lupton and Place, Trafalgar Street.

154. *(right)* War Weapons Week at Padiham, April 1941. The townsfolk raised £113,575, nearly three times more than their target of £40,000—which, incidentally, was exactly what it had cost to build the Town Hall where this photograph was taken. It was opened in 1938.

155.   Bankhouse, *c*.1906, shortly before its demolition to make way for what was the county court until early January 1989. Peter Shackleton, a local antiquarian, made the rather fantastic garden and then created a similar one behind 15 Rectory Road, where he went to live on leaving here.

156.   Cog Lane and Coalclough Lane at Gretna, *c*.1931. Cog Lane was part of the ancient highway linking Clitheroe and Rochdale, the 'limersgate', a trade route used particularly by packhorses carrying Clitheroe lime to farms in Burnley and Rossendale, then going back with coal from pits in those areas.

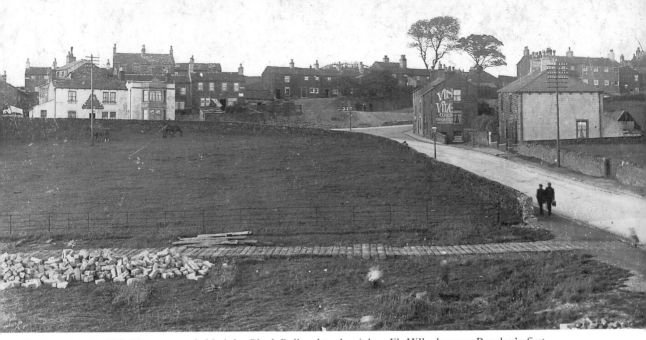

157.   Lane head, 1908. The cottages behind the *Black Bull* and to the right—Jib Hill—became Burnley's first conservation area, designated in 1971.

158.   Queen Victoria Road, 1928. Though the 1920s were hard times, Burnley acted in practical ways to resolve the situation: Thompson Park was made, the central library built, new roads made and others improved, as we see here. Slightly left of centre is Heasandford Cottage, which stood near the coke ovens at Bank Hall pit and was demolished in 1951.

159.   Sep Clough, better known as the bullfields and now part of the Parklands estate. The photograph was taken in about 1930 from the back of Rossendale Road; Bleak House and Willow Bank can be seen in the background. Burnley was a national centre for poultry-keeping between the wars and the hen-pens in the picture were typical of thousands in the district.

160.   The Mitre junction. This area takes its name from the *Mitre Inn* seen on the left of the photograph. Running into the distance is Padiham Road. All the buildings here were demolished in the 1970s when the M65 motorway was constructed.

161.   Gannow Top. This scene at the junction of Padiham Road and Gannow Lane, was another which disappeared during the construction of the motorway. Only the *Derby Inn* on the right remains today. On the right of the inn is Boat Horse Lane, which took the barge-horses over Gannow Tunnel on the Leeds and Liverpool Canal.

162.   Padiham Road. Most of the houses here were built in the 1880s. On the left is the *Tim Bobbin Inn*, named after the Lancashire poet. It is reputed that, in the early 19th century, a man sold his wife here for 2s. 6d., but repented and bought her back the next day.

163.   Ightenhill Park Lane, *c.*1908, looking towards Padiham Road. Ightenhill Park, opened in 1912, is now on the right with the bowling-greens on the left.

164.   Burnley Road, Padiham, looks little different today, but the Town Hall has now replaced Wonder Mill.

165.   Mereclough. Little different today except that the chapel on the right has gone. It was demolished in 1966 and a memorial garden now takes its place.

166.   Extwistle Hall, traditionally the home of the Parker family before they moved to Cuerden near Preston in the early 18th century. Since then, although a superb house, it has never really received the care it deserves. It was sold in October 1987 but still stands empty.

EXTWISTLE HALL

167.   Spenser's Cottage, Hurstwood, *c*.1890. Whether or not the poet Spenser ever lived at Hurstwood is open to doubt,
though there is undeniably some evidence to suggest that he did, summarised by W. A. Abram in the *Transactions of the
Burnley Literary and Scientific Club*, vol.4, 1886.

168. The Holme. Though it looks 'all of a piece', sections of it were in fact built at different times. Traditionally the home of the Whitakers, they or their close relatives lived there until 1916. It is now a residential home for the elderly.

169. Dr. T. D. Whitaker of Holme (1759-1821), vicar of that parish. He planted 400,000 trees in the Cliviger valley, built the present Holme church and wrote the *History of Whalley*, which is much wider in its scope than its title suggests. He was a man with commonsense, academic ability and practical skill.

170. Bank Hall was the home of Charlotte Ann Hargreaves, who married General Scarlett (see plate 192). Her nephew, Sir John Hardy Thursby, inherited it on her death in 1888 and was there with his family to *c*.1901. A military hospital in the First World War, it became a maternity hospital and child welfare centre in 1920, closing as such in *c*.1968 and becoming a geriatric unit until 1990. It was demolished in February/March 1993.

171. The Cannons, Colne Road. Russian guns were set up here in 1868 on land made available by the Thursbys and General Scarlett, who had used his influence with the war office to obtain the guns for Burnley. They were requisitioned for wartime scrap in October 1941.

172.   General the Hon. Sir James Yorke Scarlett, one of the few British officers to emerge with much credit from the Crimean War; he led the charge of the heavy brigade at Balaclava. With a humanity exceptional in its time, he had a concern not only for his men but for the army horses. He kept one or two in retirement in the fields at Bank Hall, his Burnley home. In 1868, he was the unsuccessful Conservative candidate in Burnley consituency's first parliamentary election.

173. Swinden House, Roggerham, *c*.1885. Two locally famous people have lived here: William Todd (1757-1842), the founder of Sunday schools in Burnley, and Tattersall Wilkinson (1825-1921), the 'sage of Roggerham', who can be seen in the doorway in this photograph.

174. The Hollins, Higher Red Lees, home of P. G. Hamerton in the 1850s and of Lady O'Hagan from 1902-21. The Hollins is now a home for the elderly.

175.   Philip Gilbert Hamerton (1834-1894), author and art critic. Though he lived in France after *c*.1861, he retained a love for the Hollins, where he had grown up: 'I often dream about it,' he wrote, 'about the old garden, the fields and the woods, the rocky streams'.

176.   Lady O'Hagan, the last resident at Towneley Hall, seen here with her young family. She involved herself very sincerely with Burnley people in all manner of good causes. She died at the Hollins in 1921 and is buried at Holme.

177.   Nos. 58a-68 Bank Parade are now all in commercial use but were built as rather fine houses *c*.1820-5, and were originally called North Parade. The name was changed in about 1876. The 'bank', incidentally, is the steep drop down to the river between the houses and St Peter's churchyard.

178.   Mrs. Mary Brown. She and her family lived at 66 Bank Parade, next door to Dr. Mackenzie, with whom her husband was in partnership. With Lady Shuttleworth she founded the Burnley House of Help in 1884; it closed as recently as 1989. She was an intelligent and energetic woman, the sort that people turn to in distress. South African by birth, she died in that country in 1935.

179.   Dr. Mackenzie, Burnley's 'beloved physician' and a renowned heart specialist, who eventually became Sir James Mackenzie, lived at 68 Bank Parade before moving to London. He is commemorated by a plaque on the house and a memorial in Thompson Park, both unveiled on the same day in September 1931.

Bibliography

Armstrong, D., *Owd Padiham* (1985)

Bennett, W., *The History of Burnley*, 4 vols. (1946-51)

Bennett, W., *The History of Burnley Grammar School* (1940)

Chapples, L., *The Taverns in the Town* (1986)

Chapples, L., *My Burnley Memories* (1993)

Frost, R. B., *A Lancashire Township: a history of Briercliffe-with-Extwistle* (1982)

Hall, B., *Burnley—a short history* (1977)

Hall, B., *Lowerhouse and the Dugdales* (1976)

Hall, B. and Frost R. B., *The Weavers' Triangle—a visitor's guide* (1983)

Lowe, J., *Burnley* (1985)

Spencer, K. G., *An Outline History of Habergham Eaves* (1989)

Thornber, T., *A Pennine Parish: the history of Cliviger* (1987)

Typescript in Burnley Central Library, Reference Department:
Nadin, J., *Notes on Collieries in the Burnley and Hapton Districts*

Local newspapers and the newspaper index in Burnley Central Library, Reference Department

The Minutes of Burnley Borough Council

Detail from an Ordnance Survey map of 1851.